Movement

by Heidi Gillis

PEARSON
Scott
Foresman

What makes things move?

Force is a push or pull.

Force may make something move.

Push the sled up a hill.

Gravity is a force.

Gravity pulls things down.

The sled goes down the hill.

The girl uses force to move the snow.

What is speed?

Push the car.

Push it with a lot of force.

It goes fast.

Speed is how fast or slow

things move.

Push the car again.

Use less force.

Now the speed of the car is slow.

Force changes how things move.

How do things move?

Things can move up and down.

Things can move left and right.

They can go straight or curve.

How else can things move?

Different Places

Look at the blocks.

Which one is on top?

Which one is on the bottom?

Which one is next to the tower?

What do magnets do?

Look at the cars.

The ends of the cars are magnets.

A **magnet** attracts some metals.

Attract means to pull toward.

A **pole** is the end of some magnets.

Magnets have a north pole.

Magnets have a south pole.

North attracts south.

North repels north.

Repel means to push away.

Pulling Metal

Iron is a kind of metal. Magnets attract things made of iron.

The magnet pulls more when it is close to something.
It pulls less when it is far away.

What will a magnet attract in this bin?

How are sounds made?

When a sound is made something vibrates.

Vibrate means to move back and forth very fast.

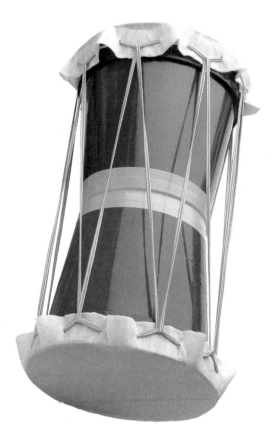

Tap the drum.

It makes a soft sound.

Hit the drum hard.

It makes a loud sound.

What sounds are around us?

Many things make sounds.

Sounds can be loud or soft.

You can hear sounds on the street.

Sounds of Nature

Sounds are all around.

Nature has sounds too.

What are ocean sounds?

Glossary

attract   to pull toward

force   a push or a pull that may make something move

gravity   a force that pulls things toward the ground

magnet   an object that attracts some metal things

pole   at the end of some magnets

repel   to push away

speed   how quickly or slowly something moves

vibrate   to move back and forth very fast